THE

LOCKSMITH

OF

LOVE

by

William S. Graham

RISING PHOENIX AUTHOR

GRAHAMR WRITINGS LLC
PUBLISHING COMPANY

The Love Locksmith/William S. Graham

ISBN-13: 978-0692176863
ISBN-10: 069217861

THE LOCKSMITH OF LOVE

I knew this feeling was right – telling myself that I'll die for it.

I'll respect it, hold it true to my heart, grow with it – enduring the rough times that occur. Keep it in my soul for greater times to come. Truly believe in what it can be. Understand the idea of its existence, beyond time. Walking with it, talking with it, and sharing something with it so precious that only true emotions can relate to it.

Knowing that the future holds moments, experiences, and memories alive in the heart, forever, I begin to see my reflection.

This is a vision – a voice – a sense of silence within.
We are all lost sheep begging to be heard by the
shepherd of words.
Quenchable collections of thoughts, ideas, feelings,
and events transpiring over time.

I started writing as a way to escape (myself) and
found myself.
For a long time, I didn't feel anything when it came love.
Emotionally numb would be the best way to describe

how I approached life and love.

Before I knew it, I was a 31-year old man with no direction in my life staring out the pale window of a state penitentiary.
I began exploring life through ink, each degree empowered my mind, and let me know more about myself.

By letting these words be your guide I ask you to question your heart. Explore the core of your soul – each part will give you the combination you need to seek happiness.

Thank you.

William S. Graham
123781
P.O. Box 392004
Denver, CO 80239

CONTENTS

Words from the Author

About The Author

ACKNOWLEDGEMENTS

My heart is warm and true thinking of you.
Special thanks to Kimberly Graham, the light of my dark situation.
When time is quiet and short of words
Just keep your head up and remember what you deserve.
When your heart breaks and all the heart aches seem to get you down
Just remember that no one can take your crown.

Special thanks to Ronald Frye and Mrs. Marilyn Boykin,
The eagle and hawk of my heart.
I fly for you and our family crest.

To all my brothas trapped in the struggle just remember we are defined by our conditions and misunderstood by our actions – vincitomnia veritas.

Special thanks to Prisons Foundation and Dennis Sobin (Director and Publisher)
'I understand what we have to do now.'

Dedicated to my beloved children Valiyah 'Jamaica'

Graham, Cyprese Lee Graham – I love you.

To Sean J. Marshall (Davinci) I am your friend and brother for life.

Goggle Young Godz Squad and witness truth. Royal Click 4 ever.

Charles 'P' Pelzer
My Brother's Keeper
Thank you,
        Salute.

A SCORE OF ZERO

You are my soul mate.

My opponent as well

My quiet purpose to never talk

My reason to yell

My divine colours within

My white canvas

unpainted My stranger in

the mist My naturally

acquainted My time to say

no My need to say yes

My subject unknown

My intelligent guess

My busy highway after work

My lonely back dirt road

My warm embrace in the winter time

My unforgettable cold

My jealous means deep down inside

My idea of never knowing the boarders wide

My score of zero from zero, added to nothing, no divide

LOVE V. S. PAIN

Heal my bleeding heart O Lord

Scuffed up by the marks of pain

Wishing to fly like the birds in the

sky But still I remain

Grounded to the ground by gravity and a thousand

pounds

Talking about being weighted down

My heart makes a blues sound

Driven across the ocean while my emotions drown

In a bottle of Tequila

With the face of a clown

My frowns are hidden behind ambitions to

smile. The mighty cloud that wouldn't rain

Pain is built up inside

Kidnapped by the years that went by

I try to maintain

But my heart is in a thousand pieces

Crumble cake and hate is not a reason

To ask why? . . . My heart is still bleeding

After all these years and tears

I remain in fear . . . .

Of love verses pain.

THE RETURN

If home was in the heart, I would be lost in the dark,

Left behind by the person I love so much,

Trapped in an image of you and his lust,

Saying to myself how could there ever be a us,

Thank you for showing me, showing me the way of

trust,

Destroy perfection with one touch,

I guess heat of passion beat you to the punch,

Only to take away from the special love we shared,

I have been haunted by the one thing I have always

feared,

But I must thank you, because you did what no other

person could do,

Brought back a player and buried a love that was true.

THE CHRONICLES OF A BROKEN HEART

FALLING APART

Here I am

At Pain Avenue

I find myself

Destroyed and mad at you

About something you didn't even consider

My feelings

Sour and bitter

Every time you litter

On my public grounds

I wither away . . . and fall down

The circus you built by hand

Made me the clown

You don't understand now

How pain can break a loyal heart

Your words winter cold

In the dark

I sat beside my dying soul

Trying to console

The pieces not having a place to go

I fall apart every time

 But this you already know . . .

Huh! Sorrow

FOREVER YOURS

My heart isn't mine

Every single beat yours to explore

To have, hold and adore

Forever more

The times of tomorrow fade away

With a slow touch of sand

Embracing the back of your hand

Under the blazing sun

I stand

Warmer

Filled with compassion

Deep in love

Always everlasting

Not caring about too much

With your love in my heart's

core I say I love you, my love,

Today, tomorrow and forever yours.

PERMANENTLY HERE

I am a tattoo upon your heart

Never removed

But moved by your essence of

love Remaining in the light of

elegance Like the angels above

Who look down on us and just smile?

Sitting on a cloud

Is where our names are written

Never forgetting

That even when it rains

We must maintain a level plain

Because pain

Has a certain place

We embrace that as one

Promising tomorrow will be better

Once we see the morning sun

And if it's not

Well at least we can say

God has given us another day

Love Locksmith   11

To kindly say

I love you Babe

Permanently here in my heart

You'll forever stay.

DRUG LOVE: PART TWO

My body ache for you in twisted ways you can only

imagine, As I fiend for you beyond any orderly fashion.

So, it's pretty safe to say that you have become my only

passion.

My meals get shorter as feelings for you grow incredible.

Like I'm willing to bet if I put cherries on skin that will

Make you even more edible, and please allow me to

elaborate

On the slow ecstasy that I can bring, because as my drug

queen

I'm planning to forever be your drug king, and with all the

Power of God from the heavens above, just know I cherish

you

With all my heart and I'm addicted to your DRUG LOVE.

A TABLE FOR TWO

I ordered the well-done crow

Marinated in lemon juice and a dozen spices

My napkin as white as a Jamaican sandy beach

A reflection in my fork as I begin to eat

It tastes alright I say!

Well that's what I tell myself in the middle of

discomfort Eating with a twisted face of ignorance

A basket of dinner rolls on every table but mine

Isn't this a perfect way to dine!

Time having no proper end to it

Loneliness having no common friend to it . . .

But me

As I truly begin to see

That a table for two

Is actually nothing without you

Now let us eat!

MY . . . ONE TRUE LOVE

Have you ever wanted someone so bad

That it hurts deep down inside?

Like a tide

Of emotions

Sweeping you over and over again

As you grin

And begin . . . . to dream of that person's glow

Because deep down inside . . . . (your heart)

You just simply know

This can grow, and truly go . . . as far as the stars are

high

"This ones all mine"

And I am blind

Like my love

Trusting the power of sight

Without a single touch

I'll continue to fight

For you . . . for us . . .

And for what I believe in (clearly)

With all my might

I'll hold this bond and love up right

For you, for me, and for us My . . .

One True Love.

ABANDONMENT

I left my heart somewhere

..... a place I can't remember at this time

I use to worry about it

Constantly it stayed on my mind

Behind

Forgot ton

Lost

From a place I can't remember at this time

Maybe somewhere on a mountain top

I didn't bother to climb

At the bottom of the ocean perhaps

In a place . . . far from here

I left my heart somewhere

Walked away . . . without shedding one tear

Life went on

I didn't say I wonder what my heart is up to now

I didn't miss it

I didn't walk around with a frown

My soul screamed . . , how you could forget your heart

somewhere,

You act as if you don't feel any resent

I just laugh at my little comments

And walk away . . . abandonment.

THERE'S NO COMPARISON

To the hear teat that constantly beats for you

I mean what is love to do

When the oceans blue

Couldn't be as deep as me and you

Finding a purpose in tomorrow

Our hands welded together through joy and times of

sorrow

Because we barrow such a love

That was made for the angles up above

They would be impressed . . . if only they could see

The depths of deep waters you swim through Just

to get to me

Because "we" . . . isn't French

It's a word we put up against

Anything and anybody who would dare try to stop this

caring and sharing

Because when it comes to my feelings for you in depth

Trust me . . . . There's No Comparison

DO YOU MIND . . . IF I MIND?

We created this foundation of love with our own

hands No fancy machines or contract builders

Just a beautiful woman and a significant man

I ask you what could be more realer?

Than working together as one . . . for one common goal

I guess the heart does know the emotions of the soul

Taking a toll on life

And paying it back with sweet memories of laughter,

joy And maybe some sorrow

Refusing to give in to the rough winds And

putting our heads up for tomorrow Saying

'please don't worry too much my Love' I

know we'll get there soon

A true journey to always remember

Like a distant trip to the moon

We saw beautiful stars there

Neither one shining like what we have

Calculated to the equation of love

And who said we were bad at math

Clearly, whoever said that

Didn't even ponder the beautiful words of time

Allowing us to build a bond beyond special

And leaving room to still read each other's mind

Do you mind . . . If I mind?

PAPER, GLASS AND STEEL

Who am I?

A jagged rock thrown against the wall

Breaking everything in sight

I died in your arms my Love And faded

away into the light Your heart

shattered like glass Now a million

pieces hit the floor Knocking with

bloody broken knuckles Hoping you

would open the door.

A folded note in my pocket

Expressing words of love and care

I ended it by saying 'I Love You'

And 'that I'll always be there.' No

air in my casket

Well at least I left a decent will

A box made of pure solid gold

Inside the box

A heart made of steel

IN THE MIST OF PAIN

I'll remain the shoulder that holds you up through

diversity

Embracing our bond as a notion to remember

What we have is special to us

A vision of a perfect love

We fit the mode as if we were made for it

And whose to say we wasn't

Maintaining in the mist of pain

We held on when we had nothing . . . but a true

promise The night having a different taste to it

A blanket of comfort . . . keeping us both warm

Outside the storm was beginning to form

A light rain drizzled upon our reflections

Your hair hanging perfectly across your face

The fate of tomorrows pain and strain soon to

come But you know what!

As I sit down and think about it

Even then we'll still be as

one In the mist of pain.

STARS

I look up
Afraid to blink
Or fade away
Thinking about you
All day
Promises fell on deaf ears
Inside I was one
Just me and my heart
Beating strong
Can't you see this sight?
I have the stars
Wet paper to the soul
They tear me apart
Every time i see them
I hate the reflection of me
They tell me where I really should be
Beside you . . . looking up
Each one unique, but only one called ours
Only one this deep
Saying sleep well my love as angels always
does You're never alone when looking at those
stars Trust me I have them to Without you

I find it truly amazing how looking up at the stars can provoke such feelings. For me it happens to be a sense of missing love. It seems like only a couple of years ago we were staring at the stars together, caught up in the daze of atonement. We didn't ask for nothing but a clear view beyond the fraction of love. It was like a mural that God painted especially for us. Now when I look at those same stars without her I feel alone and not amazed at all. 'Cherish the days of joy and chase the elements of truth!'

LOOK AT ME

The glass cuts deep

I hate these eyes

I can't sleep

I hate guys who break hearts

Take hearts for fun

Tell me I'm beautiful

Then they run

None of them understand

How I planned on killing myself

A hand full of pills

   I'm willing myself to death

Oil and blood thick

I hate these eyes

He died quick

My heart just lies there,

As if he would care once he got up

I say I love you

Nothing back

His face knots up

Leaving again – silent cries

The glass cuts deep

I hate these eyes

      Look at me!

'I broke her heart with neglect and disrespect. Sorry!

EXCUSE ME IF I GET TOO DEEP

A coat of your tenderness wrapped around my heart

Such a monsoon . . . you cover every piece of me

Satellite dishes never seen a sight so high, suddenly,

My thigh your knee to me

You ask the question . . .

What is free to me?

Free is the equate value of peace and love

Twisting your tongue in the dryer fast

You can only speak of . . .

Something so sweet honey would be jealous to know

That something this sweet was designed to grow

How low you fall

I never let you touch the ground at all

Just call . . . my name in between your peaceful sleep

And I'll be there to bow and simply say . . .

Excuse me if I get too deep.

FOR YOU

My heart is a door (saying)

Please don't knock

Just twist the gold knob It's never

locked . . . for you My soul is the

ocean's blue Something you can lose

your eyes too And truly swim

through Only

    For you . . .

Do I feel this depth of peace?

Complete . . . and batteries sold separately

For you

Perfect I may never be

But as long as you can always see . . .

My heart is loyal, true, and forever new

For you and only you.

LOVE HANGOVER – PART II

When I can't have you

    I seem to itch on a daily

basis Closing my eyes slowly

    It's amazing how I can see you in different

places.

Needing you so badly

    My veins seem to ache from pain

Trying to focus on something besides you

    I still whisper your name.

I went to all the classes

    I don't think they can help me anymore

Because every time you call for me

    I always run right out the door.

Search for what I loss then

Giving all to get it back now

Head pounding like tomorrows pain

Refusing to lay it down.

CAPTURE THE MOMENT

My words are a ship

Able to sail you away from this pain and

strain Letting you remain

In magnificent glory . . . like you came

25 / 8

I forever stand . . . as your man . .

By your side . . . looking into your eyes

Now you can rise like the morning sun

Over the midnight tide.

How beautiful you are to me?

I smile for no reason at all.

A permanent string connected to your heart

I refuse to let you fall

A kiss for each second gone

Our adversary written in stone,

Along with another kiss and hug

Saying that 'we can hold on'

Because your love is real and always true

So what can I say or do,

But capture the moment . . .

Between me and you forever

A BEAT AWAY FROM LOVE

If I could give you one thing in this world
It would be my beating heart
Literally my beating heart
Every single part . . . yours to explore
When I have nothing else to give you
Some way I'll find a way to give you more
The door wouldn't need a lock
Open to you at all times
Take your coat off and kick your feet up
I promise I don't mind
For this is yours to adore
The core of my soul completely and whole
I know you can understand when I say
I have a heart of gold
Especially knowing love is an element that grows in
your back yard
Decorating the distant pain with forgotten beauty
Massaging the scars with every finger I have
And begging you to talk to me
But not just any talk

More like a conversation between two hearts

What would be said?

If they could speak out loud

I don't know . . . . shall we listen to the hearts to find out.

TRULY, I

Smile when you smile

Holding my laugh at bay

Keeping the words you say

Under a dragon's wing

The fire never goes away

Today

      Tomorrow

           and

                Forever

You make me better

Together

We are strong

Through any weather

We hold on

Until the earth is gone

We know this to be true

But mostly

We definitely know

Truly, I love you.

WINDOW SOUL

I wrote this poem while looking out the window,

You ask me what did I see?

A world where I didn't exist called free,

The wind danced sand storms across the plain,

The mountains stood militant soldiers on a rough

terrain,

I watched the blazing sun make an enemy if the rain,

Developing a hate pattern over years of weather

change,

The trees had fun as they slow dragged to their own

beat,

Amused by watching the snowflakes dodge the

scorching heat,

Wrote this poem while looking out the window

You ask me what did I see? A world where I didn't

exist, But my soul desires to be . . . called free.

BOOK TITLE

I DON'T KNOW MY MOM

Do you know mom?

I don't

I wish I did

But as a kid – she was gone

Not gone as invisible

More like fading to show up

Especially when I needed her

Afraid of the dark

I'm hungry

Take me to the park

Church on Sunday

Tell me to be strong

Nope, she wasn't there

Sharing no memories

No local fairs

Just stares

From the adoption agency of course

I put my hand on my face

Sitting there – on the porch

Love Locksmith

Wading

To know my mom

"The greatest of faults is to be conscious of none"
— Thomas Carlye

HARMONY

As the sun comes up

I guarantee you my hand

In a condition called beauty

The birds sing to you

Simultaneously we smile

Laying in a cloud

Time . . . a pin needle to sound

We dance in thought

Consider the puddles they say

Parallel to rain drops

Looking for brighter days

I can't stop – looking at you

Fundamental tones

Overlapping consecutive motions

We stand still alone

As keys on boards

In perfect harmony

Love Locksmith

I hear you loud

Telling me to play your favourite tune

I look at you and smile

BEAUTIFUL STRANGE

Like a river to a water fall
I call you giantess
Not because you're tall
(All that is love is in you)
Purple and blue
The hue of true
Soaked in a bucket and drained for two
Yours and mine alike Waiting

To shine right
Needling to be honest and true
I don't put my faith in people
I put my faith in you –
You see light from eyes that have embrace the dark
You understand the elements of being broken by
mended hearts
You separate reality from illusion in a cruel cold world
You cherish the stone of will power as most people
would cherish a pearl
You believe in fate, but allow destiny to run its proper
course
You let love flow through your heart
With your soul being it's feeding source
You fight for truth when all the chips are down
You refuse to quit on love and keep fighting each and

every found

You show the world what madness truly should be You
sacrifice your inner – self so that your love ones can
always see

You hold time in one hand and pain the other

You show the world what it means to be a love from
the gutter

You are divine

And that's something even you can't
change Your possibilities of love are
limitless Forever

You will remain

Beautiful strange

BUTTERFLIES DON'T FLY

Consider me blessed

I know a butterfly that doesn't fly – she glides

Almost like the midnight tides

Watching over me at all times

I respect her essence

I honour her praise

I sit back and watch her strength

Adopting her ways

Lighting in a bottle

Seeing her is a beautiful sight

Holding her in my hands

Wings so lite

Colourful and always bright

Beyond her struggles deep down inside

Consider me lucky, my friend

I know a butterfly that doesn't fly – she glides

Thank you for being something you could never help being . . . **beautiful**

THE SHOVEL

We are born naked – confused
From dirt our emotions exposed
Abused
The fuse of our hearts
Beating strongly so
We dig and we dig
Afraid to let anyone know
We are scared at times
The world tells us 'you must be brave'
Telling us how to think
Showing us how to behave
Trapped in a paradox – with our own thoughts
Making us slaves
Tainted souls beyond divided notions
Silently we crave
Love . . . truth . . . time . . . trust . . . honour . . .
compassion . . .
money . . . lust . . . the grave Defined by
the dirt we come from Each layer in life
is just another level Digging up our
bones with a pot of gold I hand you . . .
the shovel – dig

WORDS FROM THE AUTHOR:

MARCUS AURELIUS

"Time fits our nature, not only because it heals griefs and quarrels, but because time's perpetual flow washes away the desperate ennui men suffer when they feel themselves imprisoned in the present."

As the world slowly turns I believe we've grown to forget the true elements of love altogether. Love has a very strong hand in the balance of hope, but that hand must be strengthened in order to fully grasp the essence of time.

I took a few years to study love and hate – reading books, understanding people and growing (what I found was shocking in fact). We detest what we don't know because it's in our best interest to trust, believe and love the things we do know.

I don't have all the answer when it comes to love, but I do know we hop for all the answers we don't want.

Love - ca va sans dire

"We can't let true love die"

Williams S. Graham
A.K.A.
KINUS KUTSUNE

Born in Anderson, SC, William S. Graham is an incarcerated author currently in Colorado Dept. of Corrections. He is the first handpicked author to be published under GrahamR Writings' new "Phoenix Rising Program. While being incarcerated, he has written over 34 books which includes an autobiography, poetry books, and two self-help books on how to help and heal yourself. He's also taken and graduated from 27 classes, attained his G.E.D. as well as earned a countless amount of good chronology recordings from the administration at his facility.

He works at the prison infirmary taking care of the sick and dying inmates during the week. This inspired him to also become certified as a CNA, which allowed him to gather more knowledge to apply to his field of work. For the last five years, on his off days, he volunteers as a Peer Educator in a program only allotted to 13 handpicked inmates and backed by the warden.

With his writings he wishes to inspire, evoke change while helping others to become better. He has also secured a 4-book deal with GrahamR Writings Publishing company to start in the following year.

Stay Tuned!

www.ingramcontent.com/pod-product-compliance
Lightning Source LLC
Chambersburg PA
CBHW071428040426
42445CB00012BA/1294